the easter experience ™

PARTICIPANT'S GUIDE

the easter experience ™

PARTICIPANT'S GUIDE

THOMAS NELSON
Since 1798

NASHVILLE   DALLAS   MEXICO CITY   RIO DE JANEIRO   BEIJING

Published in Nashville, Tennessee, by Thomas Nelson. Thomas Nelson is a
registered trademark of Thomas Nelson, Inc.

The publishers are grateful to Ross Brodfuehrer for his collaboration and writing
skills in developing the content for this book.

Thomas Nelson, Inc. titles may be purchased in bulk for educational,
business, fund-raising, or sales promotional use. For information, please e-mail
SpecialMarkets@ThomasNelson.com.

Scripture quotations are taken from the HOLY BIBLE: NEW
INTERNATIONAL VERSION®. Copyright © 1973, 1978, 1984 by
International Bible Society. Used by permission of Zondervan Publishing House.
All rights reserved.

ISBN: 978-1-4185-3400-4

Printed in the United States of America
09 10 11 12 13 RRD 6 5 4 3 2 1

contents

introduction

The Easter Experience is meant to be just that: an experience.

An experience is not something we simply read or comprehend. An experience is something that we, well . . . experience!

We *feel* an experience. We *meet* an experience. We *enter* an experience. Maybe more accurately, an experience enters *us.*

During the Easter Experience we will *feel . . . meet . . . enter* the last few hours of Jesus' natural life as well as the first few hours of His resurrected life. We will find ourselves reclining next to Him in the Upper Room, walking beside Him in Gethsemane, standing near Him in Pilate's courtyard, weeping alongside Him at Golgotha, and celebrating with Him at the empty tomb.

As we shadow Jesus, we will often find ourselves identifying with those around Him—Peter, Judas, Mary, and others. But most of all we will find ourselves identifying with Jesus Himself. And that's a good thing because the more we identify with Jesus, the more we will become like Him. For Christianity is not simply following rules; it is following Christ. And Christianity is not merely knowing about Christ; it is knowing Christ Himself. For Christianity is "Christ in you, the hope of glory" (Colossians 1:27).

*my life
has a purpose*

OPENING QUESTIONS

If people were asked to give a one- or two-word description of you, what might it be? Fun loving? Hardworking? Family oriented? Good-looking?

Watch DVD episode.

DISCUSSION

1. What are your thoughts or reactions after watching this episode?

2. This episode challenged us to make our purpose in life to be a servant of others. But why would anyone choose to be a servant?

3. Would you say you are a servant? Why or why not?

4. What is it like for you when you serve others? How does it feel?

What is it like for you when you don't serve?

Which experience is better, and why?

5. Have you found it to be true that when we really know our purpose in life, and that purpose is something beyond ourselves, then we experience the greatest fulfillment?

What life purposes have you found to be most fulfilling?

What does that fulfillment feel like?

6. Read Mark 10:35–45.

> 35 Then James and John, the sons of Zebedee, came to
> him. "Teacher," they said, "we want you to do for us
> whatever we ask." 36 "What do you want me to do for
> you?" he asked.
>
> 37 They replied, "Let one of us sit at your right and the
> other at your left in your glory." 38 "You don't know what
> you are asking," Jesus said. "Can you drink the cup I drink
> or be baptized with the baptism I am baptized with?"
>
> 39 "We can," they answered. Jesus said to them, "You will
> drink the cup I drink and be baptized with the baptism I
> am baptized with, 40 but to sit at my right or left is not for
> me to grant. These places belong to those for whom they
> have been prepared."
>
> 41 When the ten heard about this, they became indignant
> with James and John. 42 Jesus called them together and
> said, "You know that those who are regarded as rulers
> of the Gentiles lord it over them, and their high officials
> exercise authority over them. 43 Not so with you. Instead,
> whoever wants to become great among you must be your
> servant, 44 and whoever wants to be first must be slave of
> all. 45 For even the Son of Man did not come to be served,
> but to serve, and to give his life as a ransom for many."

What stands out to you from this passage?

FOR REFLECTION

Read this passage from John 13 every day this week, first asking Jesus to open your eyes to what He wants you to see. Circle, underline, or write in the margins whatever words, phrases, or thoughts stand out to you.

[1] It was just before the Passover Feast. Jesus knew that the time had come for him to leave this world and go to the Father. Having loved his own who were in the world, he now showed them the full extent of his love. [2] The evening meal was being served, and the devil had already prompted Judas Iscariot, son of Simon, to betray Jesus. [3] Jesus knew that the Father had put all things under his power, and that he had come from God and was returning to God; [4] so he got up from the meal, took off his outer clothing, and wrapped a towel around his waist. [5] After that, he poured water into a basin and began to wash his disciples' feet, drying them with the towel that was wrapped around him. [6] He came to Simon Peter, who said to him, "Lord, are you going to wash my feet?" [7] Jesus replied, "You do not realize now what I am doing, but later you will understand." [8] "No," said Peter, "you shall never wash my feet." Jesus answered, "Unless I wash you, you have no part with me." [9] "Then, Lord," Simon Peter replied, "not just my feet but my hands and my head as well!" [10] Jesus answered, "A person who has had a bath needs only to wash his feet; his whole body is clean. And you are clean, though not every one of you." [11] For he knew who was going to betray him, and that was why he said not every one was clean. [12] When he had finished washing their feet, he put on his clothes and returned to his place. "Do you understand what I have done for you?" he asked them. [13] "You call me 'Teacher' and 'Lord,' and rightly so, for that is what I am. [14] Now that I, your Lord

and Teacher, have washed your feet, you also should wash one another's feet. [15] I have set you an example that you should do as I have done for you. [16] I tell you the truth, no servant is greater than his master, nor is a messenger greater than the one who sent him. [17] Now that you know these things, you will be blessed if you do them."

NOTES

my life can change

OPENING QUESTIONS

Last week we focused on the fact that Jesus lived His earthly life as a servant. We also looked at His teachings that tell us that our purpose in life is to be servants as well. Did that lesson have any impact on how you lived out your week? If so, how?

Watch DVD episode.

DISCUSSION

1. What was your favorite part of this episode?

2. How do you see other people typically dealing with their regrets?

What have you learned from how they handled their remorse?

3. Bring to mind one of your regrets in life. You don't have to tell the group what it is, but how did you deal with it once you saw your mistake and felt the regret?

4. Kyle said the difference between remorse and repentance is that mere remorse leads one to turn to self in an attempt to make up for the mistake while repentance leads one to turn to Jesus for mercy. How would you describe the phrase "turning to Jesus" to someone who didn't know what that meant?

5. Why don't people take their regrets to Jesus first rather than try to handle those regrets by themselves?

6. When you fail or fall short, where do you tend to turn first—to yourself to fix it or to Jesus to forgive it?

How does each route usually work out over time?

7. Do you have any regrets affecting your spirit these days? Is there anything you feel badly about? Maybe it's something having to do with your marriage and how you treat your spouse. Or maybe it's something having to do with your kids. Maybe it's something having to do with money or work. Have you made some bad decisions you now regret? Try to be specific. What are you currently regretting in life?

Bring one regret to mind. If you have several, just choose one. As you think of this regret, consider where you are turning with the disappointment. Is it to self, to try to fix it? Are you trying to make up for this failure?

Imagine taking this regret to Jesus right now, as Peter did. Can you imagine saying to Him, "Lord, I am so sorry for this action"?

Now imagine His reaction to your words. What do you think it would be?

Is that reaction like His reaction to Peter's denial or it more harsh or unforgiving? If it is more harsh, why would Jesus be harder on you than He was on Peter, who had spent seen Jesus' miracles and heard His teaching, yet denied Him?

Can you picture Jesus welcoming you? Can you hear Him say, "I don't condemn you"? Can you hear Him say, "Come, let's eat together and restore our fellowship"? Can you hear Him say, "I can make all things work for the good of those who love the Father and are called to His purpose"? Picture Him saying these things to you—not because you deserve to hear them, but because He is good, and His love endures forever.

Since it is so important to make sure we are taking our regrets to the right person, let's have a time of reflection before we end our gathering. If you would, bow your head and close your eyes while we have an open time of prayer, which simply means if you would like to pray, feel free to at any time. If you would like to say something to Jesus aloud, then by all means do so.

FOR REFLECTION

Read this passage from John 20:30–21:19 every day for a week, first asking Jesus to open your eyes to what He wants you to see. Circle, underline, or write in the margins whatever words, phrases, or thoughts stand out.

20:30 Jesus did many other miraculous signs in the presence of his disciples, which are not recorded in this book. 31 But these are written that you may believe that Jesus is the Christ, the Son of God, and that by believing you may have life in his name. 21:1 Afterward Jesus appeared again to his disciples, by the Sea of Tiberias. It happened this way: 2 Simon Peter, Thomas (called Didymus), Nathanael from Cana in Galilee, the sons of Zebedee, and two other disciples were together. 3 "I'm going out to fish," Simon Peter told them, and they said, "We'll go with you." So they went out and got into the boat, but that night they caught nothing. 4 Early in the morning, Jesus stood on the shore, but the disciples did not realize that it was Jesus. 5 He called out to them, "Friends, haven't you any fish?" "No," they answered. 6 He said, "Throw your net on the right side of the boat and you will find some." When they did, they were unable to haul the net in because of the large number of fish. 7 Then the disciple whom Jesus loved said to Peter, "It is the Lord!" As soon as Simon Peter heard him say, "It is the Lord," he wrapped his outer garment around him (for he had taken it off) and jumped into the water. [8] The other disciples followed in the boat, towing the net full of fish, for they were not far from shore, about a hundred yards. [9] When they landed, they saw a fire of burning coals there with fish on it, and some bread. [10] Jesus said to them, "Bring some of the fish you have just caught." [11] Simon Peter climbed aboard and dragged the net ashore. It was full of large fish, 153, but even with so many the net was not torn. [12] Jesus said to them, "Come and have breakfast." None of the disciples dared ask him, "Who are you?" They knew it was the Lord. [13] Jesus came, took the bread and gave it to them, and did the same with the fish. [14] This was now the third time Jesus appeared to his disciples after he was raised from the dead. [15] When they had finished eating, Jesus said to Simon Peter, "Simon son of John, do you truly love me more than these? "Yes, Lord," he said, "you know that I love you." Jesus said, "Feed my lambs." [16] Again Jesus said, "Simon son of John, do you truly love me?" He answered, "Yes, Lord, you know that I love you." Jesus said, "Take care of my sheep." [17] The third time he said to him, "Simon son of John, do you love me?" Peter was hurt because Jesus asked him the third time, "Do you love me?" He said, "Lord, you know all things; you know that I love you." Jesus said, "Feed my sheep. [18] I tell you the truth, when you were younger you dressed yourself and went where you wanted; but when you are old you will stretch out your hands, and someone else will dress you and lead you where you do not want to go." [19] Jesus said this to indicate the kind of death by which Peter would glorify God. Then he said to him, "Follow me!"

my pain is understood

OPENING QUESTIONS

Have you ever gone through something painful or difficult, and felt as though no one understood what you were going through? How would you describe what that was like?

Have you ever gone through something hard, but had someone alongside you who had gone through something similar him- or herself? What was that like?

Watch DVD episode.

DISCUSSION

1. This episode focuses heavily on the sufferings of Jesus—the emotional and relational sufferings to be sure—but especially the physical agony, and that suffering is very graphic. How do you feel about so much focus on the physical trials of Jesus?

2. The episode referred to a letter in the New Testament called Hebrews. Read Hebrews 1:1–4. Listen for what this writer says about Jesus:

> [1] In the past God spoke to our forefathers through the prophets at many times and in various ways, [2] but in these last days he has spoken to us by his Son, whom he appointed heir of all things, and through whom he made the universe. [3] The Son is the radiance of God's glory and the exact representation of his being, sustaining all things by his powerful word. After he had provided purification for sins, he sat down at the right hand of the Majesty in heaven. [4] So he became as much superior to the angels as the name he has inherited is superior to theirs.

What do you notice about Jesus in these verses?

3. Read Hebrews 2:10–11.

> [10] In bringing many sons to glory, it was fitting that
> God, for whom and through whom everything exists,
> should make the author of their salvation perfect through
> suffering. [11] Both the one who makes men holy and those
> who are made holy are of the same family. So Jesus is not
> ashamed to call them brothers.

What does it say that suffering did for Jesus?

How could Jesus be made perfect through suffering?

Wasn't He perfect already? What was He lacking before He took on flesh and endured suffering?

4. What is the consequence of Jesus' sufferings in regard to His relationship with us, as described in verse 11?

5. Read Hebrews 2:14–18. Again, look for what comes out of Jesus' sufferings.

> ¹⁴ Since the children have flesh and blood, he too shared in their humanity so that by his death he might destroy him who holds the power of death—that is, the devil— ¹⁵ and free those who all their lives were held in slavery by their fear of death.
> ¹⁶ For surely it is not angels he helps, but Abraham's descendants. ¹⁷ For this reason he had to be made like his brothers in every way, in order that he might become a merciful and faithful high priest in service to God, and that he might make atonement for the sins of the people. ¹⁸ Because he himself suffered when he was tempted, he is able to help those who are being tempted.

6. Can you think of any kind of suffering to which Jesus could not relate?

7. Do you think Jesus really knows how you feel? Does He truly relate to whatever hardships you are going through?

8. How does all we've discussed and viewed in the last few minutes impact you? What difference does it make to you?

FOR REFLECTION

Read the following passages from Hebrews every day this week, first asking Jesus to open your eyes to what He wants you to see. Circle, underline, or write in the margins whatever words, phrases, or thoughts stand out.

> [1:1] In the past God spoke to our forefathers through the prophets at many times and in various ways, [2] but in these last days he has spoken to us by his Son, whom he appointed heir of all things, and through whom he made the universe. [3] The Son is the radiance of God's glory and the exact representation of his being, sustaining all things by his powerful word. After he had provided purification for sins, he sat down at the right hand of the Majesty in heaven. [4] So he became as much superior to the angels as the name he has inherited is superior to theirs.

2:10 In bringing many sons to glory, it was fitting that God, for whom and through whom everything exists, should make the author of their salvation perfect through suffering. 11 Both the one who makes men holy and those who are made holy are of the same family. So Jesus is not ashamed to call them brothers.

2:14 Since the children have flesh and blood, he too shared in their humanity so that by his death he might destroy him who holds the power of death—that is, the devil— 15 and free those who all their lives were held in slavery by their fear of death. 16 For surely it is not angels he helps, but Abraham's descendants. 17 For this reason he had to be made like his brothers in every way, in order that he might become a merciful and faithful high priest in service to God, and that he might make atonement for the sins of the people. 18 Because he himself suffered when he was tempted, he is able to help those who are being tempted.

4:14 Therefore, since we have a great high priest who has gone through the heavens, Jesus the Son of God, let us hold firmly to the faith we profess. 15 For we do not have a high priest who is unable to sympathize with our weaknesses, but we have one who has been tempted in every way, just as we are—yet was without sin. 16 Let us then approach the throne of grace with confidence, so that we may receive mercy and find grace to help us in our time of need.

NOTES

my life has a plan

OPENING QUESTION

 When you were little, what did you dream of being or doing when you grew up?

Watch DVD episode.

DISCUSSION

1. How has your life been different from what you expected?

2. What do people usually expect in life?

What don't they expect?

What leads people to expect life to be fairly smooth and easy?

3. Do you see any difference in what believers in Jesus expect in life and what nonbelievers expect?

4. The most common reason people turn their backs on God is because He doesn't do something they expect He should, such as heal their best friend or stop the bus accident that killed their daughter. What can we expect from God?

5. If God will let His own Son not only die but also suffer horrifically, what does that imply about our lives?

6. Read each of the scriptures below. Have you ever seen these verses on a plaque or a greeting card, or have you ever personally tried to memorize them?

- "Ask and it will be given to you; seek and you will find; knock and the door will be opened to you. For everyone who asks receives; he who seeks finds; and to him who knocks, the door will be opened" (Matthew 7:7–8).

- "But seek first his kingdom and his righteousness, and all these things will be given to you as well" (Matthew 6:33).

- "I have come that they may have life, and have it to the full" (John 10:10).

- "Dear friends, do not be surprised at the painful trial you are suffering, as though something strange were happening to you. But rejoice that you participate in the sufferings of Christ, so that you may be overjoyed when his glory is revealed" (1 Peter 4:12–13).

- "Now if we are children, then we are heirs—heirs of God and co-heirs with Christ, if indeed we share in his sufferings in order that we may also share in his glory" (Romans 8:17).

- "For it has been granted to you on behalf of Christ not only to believe on him, but also to suffer for him" (Philippians 1:29).

Why don't we put verses like these last three on plaques or memorize them?

Would it be good for us to do so?

FOR REFLECTION

Read these three New Testament passages every day this week, first asking Jesus to open your eyes to what He wants you to see. Circle, underline, or write in the margins whatever words, phrases, or thoughts stand out.

Dear friends, do not be surprised at the painful trial you are suffering, as though something strange were happening to you. But rejoice that you participate in the sufferings of Christ, so that you may be overjoyed when his glory is revealed. (1 Peter 4:12–13)

Now if we are children, then we are heirs—heirs of God and co-heirs with Christ, if indeed we share in his sufferings in order that we may also share in his glory. (Romans 8:17)

For it has been granted to you on behalf of Christ not only to believe on him, but also to suffer for him. (Philippians 1:29)

NOTES

I have the promise of eternal life

OPENING QUESTIONS

 Have you ever known anyone who ended up in jail? If so, what was their story?

 Do you identify with that person in any way?

Watch DVD episode.

DISCUSSION

1. Rembrandt painted himself into his portrayal of the crucifixion. If you were to paint yourself into the scene, where would you be? What would you be doing?

2. Of all the characters we've looked at—such as these two thieves, Peter, Judas, Mary—or even of those we haven't looked at closely, like John or the soldiers, with whom do you most identify and why?

3. This episode focused a great deal on the one criminal. What is it that leads a person to steal what someone else has and use it for himself?

4. We might wonder how a man could end up as a habitual crook. But is there a sin you commit habitually? Maybe it is gossiping—after all, what's so wrong about that? Or maybe lusting—it's impossible to prevent anyway, right? Or simply living for yourself—after all, doesn't everybody?

When you end up doing the same wrong thing over and over, what effect does it have on you?

What effect does it have on your relationship with Christ?

5. Something Jesus said or did changed the criminal, though we don't know what it was. What changed you? What did Jesus say or do that originally led you to turn toward Him?

6. We sometimes hear, "Even if you were the only person on earth, Jesus would have died for you." If you were the only one, are your wrongs so bad that Jesus would have to die for you?

7. Let's look at one passage from the second chapter of James. James, the brother of Jesus, did not come to believe that Jesus was the Messiah until after His resurrection. Read verses 8–11.

> [8] If you really keep the royal law found in Scripture, "Love your neighbor as yourself," you are doing right. [9] But if you show favoritism, you sin and are convicted by the law as lawbreakers. [10] For whoever keeps the whole law and yet stumbles at just one point is guilty of breaking all of it. [11] For he who said, "Do not commit adultery," also said, "Do not murder." If you do not commit adultery but do commit murder, you have become a lawbreaker.

Here we are told that whoever falters at one point of the law, even something as "small" as showing favoritism to one person over another, is guilty of breaking all the law. What do you make of that?

FOR REFLECTION

Read this passage from Luke 18 every day this week, first asking Jesus to open your eyes to what He wants you to see. Circle, underline, or write in the margins whatever words, phrases, or thoughts stand out.

⁹ To some who were confident of their own righteousness and looked down on everybody else, Jesus told this parable:
¹⁰ "Two men went up to the temple to pray, one a Pharisee and the other a tax collector. ¹¹ The Pharisee stood up and prayed about himself: 'God, I thank you that I am not like other men—robbers, evildoers, adulterers—or even like this tax collector. ¹² I fast twice a week and give a tenth of all I get.'
¹³ "But the tax collector stood at a distance. He would not even look up to heaven, but beat his breast and said, 'God, have mercy on me, a sinner.' ¹⁴ I tell you that this man, rather than the other, went home justified before God. For everyone who exalts himself will be humbled, and he who humbles himself will be exalted."

NOTES

my hope is secure

OPENING QUESTIONS

 What do you think is the saddest word in the dictionary?

 What is the happiest word?

Watch DVD episode.

DISCUSSION

1. What scene in today's DVD episode did you like the best?

What was it about that scene that struck you?

If you really believed what that scene communicated, how would it or should it impact your life?

2. Have you ever personally experienced the word *hopeless?*

How would you describe it?

How was your hope restored?

3. Why does God allow us times of seeming hopelessness?

4. Kyle names three assurances that come from Jesus rising from the dead.

   a. We can be confident that Jesus will do what He says He will do.

   b. We can be confident in our relationship with God.

   c. We can be confident Jesus will come back for us.

   Which of these assurances means the most to you?

   What is the most telling evidence for you that Jesus actually did rise from the dead?

5. Read verses 50–58 in 1 Corinthians 15, often called the Resurrection Chapter.

> [50] I declare to you, brothers, that flesh and blood cannot inherit the kingdom of God, nor does the perishable inherit the imperishable. [51] Listen, I tell you a mystery: We will not all sleep, but we will all be changed— [52] in a flash, in the twinkling of an eye, at the last trumpet. For the trumpet will sound, the dead will be raised imperishable, and we will be changed.
> [53] For the perishable must clothe itself with the imperishable, and the mortal with immortality. [54] When the perishable has been clothed with the imperishable, and the mortal with immortality, then the saying that is written will come true: "Death has been swallowed up in victory."
> [55] "Where, O death, is your victory? Where, O death, is your sting?" [56] The sting of death is sin, and the power of sin is the law. [57] But thanks be to God! He gives us the victory through our Lord Jesus Christ. [58] Therefore, my dear brothers, stand firm. Let nothing move you. Always give yourselves fully to the work of the Lord, because you know that your labor in the Lord is not in vain.

Look over those words. Paul certainly believed those truths. He not only suffered for them but was executed for them. How would you like those words, those truths, to impact your everyday life?

FOR REFLECTION

Read this passage from 1 Corinthians 15 every day this week,
first asking Jesus to open your eyes to what He wants you to see.
Circle, underline, or write in the margins whatever words, phrases,
or thoughts stand out.

⁵⁰ I declare to you, brothers, that flesh and blood cannot
inherit the kingdom of God, nor does the perishable inherit
the imperishable. ⁵¹ Listen, I tell you a mystery: We will not
all sleep, but we will all be changed— ⁵² in a flash, in the
twinkling of an eye, at the last trumpet. For the trumpet will
sound, the dead will be raised imperishable, and we will be
changed.
⁵³ For the perishable must clothe itself with the imperishable,
and the mortal with immortality. ⁵⁴ When the perishable has
been clothed with the imperishable, and the mortal with
immortality, then the saying that is written will come true:
"Death has been swallowed up in victory." ⁵⁵ "Where, O
death, is your victory? Where, O death, is your sting?" ⁵⁶ The
sting of death is sin, and the power of sin is the law. ⁵⁷ But
thanks be to God! He gives us the victory through our Lord
Jesus Christ. ⁵⁸ Therefore, my dear brothers, stand firm. Let
nothing move you. Always give yourselves fully to the work of
the Lord, because you know that your labor in the Lord is not
in vain.

CPSIA information can be obtained at www.ICGtesting.com
Printed in the USA
LVOW08s2353140115

422704LV00006B/26/P